DAVID AND GOLIATH

ISBN: 1-56173-720-8

Contributing Writer: Marlene Targ Brill

Consultant: David M. Howard, Jr., Ph.D.

Cover Illustration: Stephen Marchesi

Book Illustrations: Thomas Gianni

David M. Howard, Jr., Ph.D. is an associate professor of Old Testament
and Semitic Languages, and is a member of the Society of Biblical
Literature and the Institute for Biblical Research.

Publications International, Ltd.

Long ago in the town of Bethlehem, there lived a boy named David. He was a handsome, young shepherd boy. More important than how he looked on the outside, David was beautiful on the inside. God knew this and watched over him.

David and his eight brothers were all sons of Jesse. Everyday when David would go to tend the sheep, he would grab his shepherd's staff and harp. With a quick wave to his father, David would be off to watch the sheep. He would play the harp to calm the sheep and help make the day go by faster.

Nearby in Bethlehem lived Saul, the king of Israel. Saul was an unhappy man. At one time he had loved and respected God. But then one day Saul displeased God. After that, Saul became very sad.

One day when Saul felt sad, a servant suggested that they find someone to play the harp for him. The music might make the king feel better. Saul thought it was a good idea. Another servant knew David and suggested he play for the king.

They asked Jesse, David's father, if it would be alright if David played for the king. He agreed, and David went to the palace.

David's music did make King Saul feel better. Saul wanted him to stay at the palace. So he asked Jesse, "Will you let David stay with me? He pleases me very much."

Meanwhile, David's brothers joined Saul's army. Since they were gone, David had to travel back and forth, playing his harp at the palace and tending the sheep at home. On one trip home, Jesse said, "I hear the Philistines are ready to fight. I am worried about your older brothers. Take this food to them. Then come back and let me know how they are."

David got up early the next day, picked up the sack of food, and started on the trip.

As David got near to the camp, he heard yelling. The two armies were lined up and ready to fight. He left the sack of food with a guard and went to find his brothers. As David greeted them, he heard:

"Today I dare the army of Israel." It was a giant Philistine soldier trying to make someone fight him. "Give me a man to fight. If he should win, we are your servants. If I win, you are our servants."

Saul's soldiers were afraid. This man was so big and strong. Surely no one could win a fight against him. David stepped right up and shouted, "I will fight the giant Goliath myself!"

David's brothers told him to be quiet and go home. But David would not listen. He repeated his promise to a soldier who then told King Saul. The king sent for David. "Don't be afraid," insisted David. "I will go and fight this Philistine."

"You are just a boy who tends sheep," said the king. "Goliath has been a warrior since he was a child."

"I know I am a shepherd boy," admitted David. But he told the king how he had rescued sheep from bears and lions. He wasn't afraid then and he wasn't afraid now. "God has saved me from both lions and bears," David told Saul. "God will save me from Goliath, too."

King Saul now knew what had to be done. "Go and may God be with you!" the king said. Saul wanted to help David, so he had heavy armor put on him. But David was not used to it. "I cannot walk with this armor," he told Saul. "It is too heavy."

David removed the armor. Walking to a nearby stream, he picked out five smooth stones. He put them in his pouch, grabbed his sling and shepherd's crook, and started off to fight the giant.

Goliath marched his huge body toward David. The sunshine glared off the large shiny helmet on the giant's head. His body was protected by heavy armor. Layers of armor covered his legs. And in Goliath's hand was a fierce looking spear that weighed over 15 pounds! The giant was truly a frightening sight.

Goliath stomped closer to David. He looked down at the creature far beneath him. He thought David was too young and small. Was someone playing a joke on him?

"Am I a dog that you come to me with sticks?" yelled the angry Philistine. "Come to me and I will feed you to the birds and wild animals."

David answered Goliath, "You come at me with a sword and spear. But I come to you in the name of God who protects the army of Israel whom you dared."

David continued, "This very day I will strike you down. Everyone will know that there is a God in Israel. And that God does not save by spear and sword."

The angry Philistine ran at David to attack him. David raced toward the battle line to meet the giant. As he went, David pulled a stone from his bag. Then he stopped, fixed the stone in his sling, and flung it mightily toward the Philistine. The stone flew through the air toward the vicious giant.

The stone struck the giant on his forehead. Goliath fell face down on the ground. The earth trembled from his weight. David ran and stood over Goliath. He grabbed the giant's sword from its case. He held the sword high to show both armies he won.

The Philistines saw that Goliath, their champion, was no more. How could even the mightiest giant try to defeat someone when God was on their side? Realizing there was no hope, they ran away with Saul's army right behind them.

David went back to Saul's tent to tell him about Goliath. When the king heard the good news, he was so happy! He knew that God was with David.

Saul thanked David for saving Israel. Saul's son, Jonathan, gave David robes and armor. David lived in the palace like a royal son.

David still played his harp for the king. But Saul made the boy a leader in his army. David won battle after battle. The people grew to know and love him. David later became king. With God's help, he won many more battles over the Philistines.

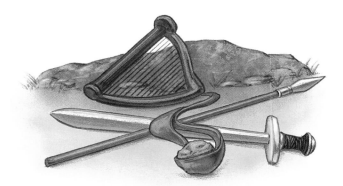